ENDANGERED SPECIES

A COLLECTION OF U.S. POSTAGE STAMPS

Endangered Species

Copyright ©1996
United States Postal Service
All rights reserved.

ISBN: 0-9644038-8-9

These stamps were produced by Stamp Services,
United States Postal Service.

Published to the trade by
ANTICS Books
1700 K Street, NW, Suite 400
Washington, DC 20006

Distributed to the trade by
Specialty Marketing Group, Inc.
41 Monroe Turnpike
Trumbell, CT 06611
Tel: 1-800-698-7781
Fax: 1-800-557-5601

Printed in the United States of America

Table of
Contents

Introduction

by Kathryn S. Fuller, President, World Wildlife Fund

CALIFORNIA CONDORS. WHOOPING CRANES. BLACK-FOOTED FERRETS. PEREGRINE FALCONS. BLUE WHALES. FLORIDA PANTHERS. ATLANTIC STURGEONS.

What do all these animals have in common? They, along with hundreds of their fellow species, are on the verge of vanishing from this planet.

They are among the hundreds of plant and animal species in the United States that are considered "endangered"—that is, in immediate danger of becoming extinct. Another large group is considered "threatened," which means they are likely to become endangered if they aren't protected. All told, nearly a thousand animal species in the United States alone are fighting for their very survival.

Why should we care if species become extinct? How could the fate of a Hawaiian monk seal or a piping plover possibly affect human beings?

To understand the importance of each individual species, we need to see how it fits into the larger puzzle. Every animal, plant, and micro-organism, every rock and clod of soil—every human being—connects to something larger, something that conservationists measure as "biodiversity." Biodiversity means not just an abundance of species, but also an abundance of ecosystems to support them—and enough genetic variety *within* species to allow them to fight off disease and adapt to changing surroundings. It means, in other words, a healthy, sustainable planet.

We all know that this Earth is blessed with an incredible array of life, ranging from single-celled organisms to 150-ton whales. Scientists have identified about 1.4 million separate species, a staggering number in itself, but one that just scratches the surface. The noted biologist E. O. Wilson has estimated that the Earth houses anywhere between 10 and 100 million species.

Tropical rain forests, by themselves, account for a good half of the species on Earth. But plant and animal species are found in every corner of the world, in temperate forests and coral reefs and wetlands, in the coldest polar regions and the hottest, driest deserts.

When we picture this incredible, interconnected web of life, we can see that the loss of any individual web strand—that is, the loss of any species—no matter how small it may be, affects the larger structure. And the more strands we lose, the more we risk losing the whole web.

Every bit of biological diversity is precious. Every species is the product of millions of years of evolution and is the storehouse of a vast wealth of genetic information.

Of course, biodiversity also provides important direct benefits to people. When we have a diversity of wild plants, for instance, we can grow better crops and produce new foods.

Nature is also a vital source of new medicines. While few people would choose to seek out a pit viper, its venom can be used in medicines to reduce blood pressure. The endangered rosy periwinkle plant from Madagascar produces chemicals that help cure leukemia and certain types of cancer. The bark of the Pacific yew tree produces an anti-cancer drug called taxol. In fact, a good quarter of all the prescription medicines in the United States have active ingredients that originally came from plants.

If we had allowed these plants to become extinct, we never would have known what healing properties they had. What's more, 95 percent of the world's plants have not even been studied yet for their use as medicines. Who knows which one of them contains an effective treatment for cancer or for AIDS?

These are just some of the ways in which biodiversity acts as our "safety net." Life sustains life. Where natural resources are depleted, people must struggle that much harder to survive. Like everything else in nature, we depend on biodiversity for our survival. Unfortunately, though, we are making it harder for other species to survive.

To a certain extent, extinction has always been a part of nature. But what concerns so many scientists now is how *quickly* extinction is happening. Dr. Wilson has estimated that we are currently losing at least *three species every hour*—more than 70 a day.

The most serious problem driving species to extinction is the *loss of habitat*. Less than 5 percent of the Earth's land surface is protected in national parks. Every day, more and more natural areas are lost to roads, houses, shopping malls, farms, and other types of human development. When people clear woods, fill in wetlands, or pave over meadows, they alter habitats—and, in the process, they kill or force out the animals and plants that once lived in these habitats, upsetting ecological relationships that may have taken millions of years to evolve.

Besides habitat loss, there are other forces causing species to go extinct:

People harm species by using too many fossil fuels or consuming forests, minerals, water, and other resources at a much faster rate than those resources can be replaced. Industrialized countries like the United States make up only a quarter of the Earth's population—but they use *three-quarters* of its resources.

Species also suffer from pollution—like an oil spill, an overflowing landfill, or something less obvious—like acid rain or the pesticides that wash into waterways that have deadly effects on animals and plants alike.

Population growth is another problem. In 1993, there were approximately 5.5 billion people on the planet, more than twice as many as there were in 1950. And every day we add about 250,000 more people. Supporting such huge numbers puts increased pressure on natural resources.

Also complicating things are introduced species—the plants and animals brought, by accident or on purpose, to places where they don't naturally occur. These new species often spread quickly, pushing out native species. One introduced tree species in Hawaii has wiped out more than 30,000 acres of native forest.

As you can see, these are all complex problems that will take time and effort to solve. But the outlook for endangered species isn't totally bleak. After decades of work, conservationists are starting to see more and more species "success stories." The Arabian oryx, for instance, at one point had vanished altogether from the wild, but now it has returned. Also making a comeback is the golden lion tamarin, a rare, squirrel-sized primate that was once on the verge of disappearing from its Brazilian forest home.

Two decades ago, the bald eagle, our national symbol, was also on its way to extinction—a victim of pesticide poisoning from DDT. But once DDT was banned in the United States and the eagle was protected under the Endangered Species Act, the bird began to make an impressive recovery and now is no longer considered endangered.

What can *you* do to save species from extinction? Quite a lot. In fact, anything you do to help the environment will have some positive impact on wildlife. Follow the example of people around the country who are starting recycling drives, promoting energy conservation, and raising money for rain forests and endangered species.

And as you look at the beautiful species in this book and read their stories, think about how your own actions may, even in the most indirect way, affect their survival. Look at the choices you make every day, the things you buy and throw away, the energy you use. Remember: we're all in this together. In fact, humans have more stake in a healthy planet than any other species.

> # To understand the importance of each individual species, we need to see how it fits into the larger puzzle.

What Zoos Can Do for
Endangered Species
by Joan Embrey, San Diego Zoo

BY FEATURING 15 ENDANGERED SPECIES ON A SHEET OF POSTAGE STAMPS, THE U. S. POSTAL SERVICE CALLS ATTENTION TO THE PLIGHT OF ALL ENDANGERED ANIMALS.

It's amazing how dramatically the world, and the role zoos play in conservation efforts, have changed since I began working for the Zoological Society of San Diego over twenty years ago.

In 1968, more than 1.5 million elephants still roamed the savannahs and forests of Africa. Today, because of poaching and habitat destruction, the number is down to 350,000 elephants.

The black rhinoceros population has dwindled—mainly because of poaching—from 65,000 animals to less than 2,000. Many other species are experiencing comparable declines in population.

Rain forests are logged for timber and farmland in South America and southern Asia. Scrubby eucalyptus groves in Australia are cut down to make way for housing developments and hotels. Coastal sage and deserts are developed in North America. A hole in the ozone layer threatens Antarctica. Humans are having an impact on natural environments all over the world. Wildlife populations are suffering because they're losing their homes.

The missions and goals of today's zoos have been broadened to address today's problems. Educating people about the biology of animals and breeding endangered species in captivity are important, but zoos are doing much, much more than that.

First and foremost, U.S. zoos and wildlife parks are joining forces with international governments and conservation organizations such as the World Wildlife Fund, the Australian Koala Foundation, the Jane Goodall Institute, and the Nature Conservancy to help save animals and their habitats. A positive future for wildlife depends upon a balance between human needs and the need to preserve habitats and ecosystems.

For example, scientists at the San Diego Zoo's Center for Reproduction of Endangered Species are working with Chinese researchers and wildlife agencies on a variety of giant panda conservation projects. Pandas are critically endangered, numbering less than 1,000 animals in the wild, and their forest habitat is fragmented. The scientists are studying all aspects of giant panda scent marking, from behavior to chemical composition. Understanding the mysteries of scent marking is important as the researchers plan boundaries for new panda reserves and establish corridors that will link reserves together.

Also, in the near future, we hope that the People's Republic of China will be loaning two giant pandas to the San Diego Zoo. Once the pandas get to San Diego, the Zoo has agreed to send $1 million per year for 12 years to China, to be used specifically for giant panda habitat preservation.

Another change in the world of zoos is the actual design of the animal exhibits. Today's zoos develop enclosures that recreate a species' native habitat. This is quite a change from thirty years ago, when a cement enclosure with a jungle gym was considered "state of the art" for gorillas. The exhibits are much better—more comfortable for the animals, and more realistic and educational for the human visitors.

In 1991, the San Diego Zoo completed Gorilla Tropics, a two-and-a-half acre simulation of African rain forest. It includes a gorilla habitat planted with trees and bushes collected from Africa, a walk-through bird aviary that features a thunderstorm every 30 minutes, and even a compact disc system that plays authentic African jungle sounds throughout the area.

The gorilla troop can climb on logs, lounge by a waterfall, nap in the shade, snack on the plants, and even retreat from the public's view if the mood strikes them. The result is a contented gorilla family; four baby gorillas have been born in Gorilla Tropics since it opened.

For human visitors, a trip through Gorilla Tropics is the next best thing to trekking through the rain forests of Africa…and a lot safer. Less expensive and more comfortable, too!

At many zoos, new exhibits are being designed to inform visitors about wildlife and conservation on a much broader scope. By immersing visitors in simulated habitats, and through innovative graphics, tours, and classes, zoos are teaching people how everything on earth—from animals to plants to human activities—are interconnected. Also, people are given specific ideas about what they personally can do to help wildlife and various ecosystems.

With better exhibits come improved opportunities for animals to breed, which creates self-sustaining populations. Also, the opportunities are better for researchers to continue gathering important biological information about the animals. The more biologists know about wildlife and their habits, the more they can assist with managing and saving wild populations of animals.

In the cases of a few species like the California condor, black-footed ferret, thick-billed parrot, and Arabian oryx, scientists have on-going programs to return animals from captivity to their native wild habitats. The key to projects such as these, though, is to make sure that there is a "wild" to which the animals can be returned.

I feel proud of what zoos and wildlife parks have been able to accomplish in the past decades. Not only has much been done in the way of conservation, but also children and adults have been given an opportunity to see animals that they would never see anywhere else. In many cases, zoos offer people their only contact with animals of any sort…even farm animals.

I invite you to support the zoo in your community and become involved in any way that you can.

On behalf of the U. S. Postal Service, I hope you will collect these beautiful stamps! To all of you—our future generation of conservationists—I invite you to support the zoo in your community and become involved in any way that you can. We must work together to preserve our wildlife heritage and the future of our planet.

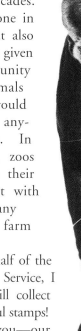

The black-footed ferret once ranged throughout the Great Plains, from Texas northward to Saskatchewan. The ferret was believed extinct when a small population was found in Wyoming in 1981. Since then, experimental populations have been reintroduced into Wyoming, Montana, and South Dakota.

Black-footec

THE BLACK-FOOTED FERRET MAY NEVER HAVE BEEN NUMEROUS, BUT IT HAS ALWAYS BEEN ELUSIVE. FIRST DESCRIBED BY NATURALISTS JOHN AUDUBON AND JOHN BACHMAN IN 1851, ANOTHER WAS NOT SIGHTED FOR 25 YEARS.

Ferrets once ranged throughout the Great Plains in populations from Texas northward to Saskatchewan. Wherever black-footed ferrets were found, there were prairie dogs nearby. This is because prairie dogs are the primary diet of the black-footed ferret; they also dig the burrows in which the ferret lives. Nocturnal members of the weasel family, ferrets are most active at night. They bound up and down and in and out of the prairie dogs' burrows in search of food. After making a kill, ferrets will often bring their catch to a favored burrow to consume it. Females often carry fresh prey to their homes, the burrows in which they care for their young.

Female black-footed ferrets have one litter per year, generally giving birth to four or five young in late spring. The kits remain underground, in the maze of burrows, until they are about six weeks old. As summer passes, the young become increasingly more independent, and by October they are ready to fend for themselves.

Because they are so dependent on prairie dogs, ferret populations rise and fall with those of its prey. (It has been estimated that it takes 100 to 150 acres of prairie dog colony to support a single black-footed ferret.) As the West was being settled, prairie dogs had to compete with live-stock for the first time. Intensive efforts were made to eradicate this "pest" from the prairies. Without the prairie dog, the black-footed ferret could not survive. Its numbers declined rapidly and, by 1967, the ferret was listed as "endangered." By 1980, it was believed extinct.

In 1981, however, a Wyoming rancher brought an unfamiliar animal that his dog had killed to a taxidermist who recognized it as a black-footed ferret.

This led to the discovery of a small population of ferrets. By 1984, nearly 130 were counted. Of these, six were selected for a captive breeding program. Shortly thereafter, all six died of a disease that was decimating the wild population. Only 18 remained in the wild, all of which were captured for a captive breeding program. These remained healthy and bred, increasing to more than 400 captive black-footed ferrets.

The black-footed ferret may, in fact, be a rare success story. Reintroduction in the wild began in 1991 in Wyoming and, subsequently, in Montana and South Dakota. Annual releases over a period of five years may take place at these sites. Areas in Utah, Colorado, and Arizona also have been identified as possible release sites, with reintroduction into Arizona likely to begin soon. By the year 2010, it is hoped that 1,500 free-ranging ferrets will be established in the wild.

The black-footed ferret may, in fact, be a rare success story.

Ferret

The thick-billed parrot is primarily a native of Mexico, but small populations once inhabited Arizona and New Mexico. By the early 1900s, due to overhunting and habitat loss, the United States population had disappeared. A few offspring of reintroduced thick-billed parrots are now struggling to survive in Arizona and New Mexico.

Thick-billed parrot

32 USA

Thick-billec

THE THICK-BILLED PARROT'S COLOR-ATION IS STRIKING: ITS PLUMAGE IS LIME GREEN AND IT HAS BRIGHT RED PATCHES ON ITS FOREHEAD AND FOREWING. A YELLOW STRIPE ON THE UNDERSIDE OF EACH WING IS VISIBLE WHEN THE BIRD IS IN FLIGHT.

It is a strong flyer that regularly reaches speeds of 50 miles per hour. Large flocks in V formation streak through the sky, easily outflying goshawks and red-tailed hawks, their primary predators.

These social parrots nest together in forests of pine and fir trees. They feed on conifer cones as well as on acorns and juniper berries.

Primarily native to Mexico, the thick-billed parrot once inhabited Arizona and New Mexico. By the early 1900s, the U.S. population of parrots had disappeared due to overhunting. The thick-billed parrot faced possible extinction because much of its habitat was destroyed by deforestation.

From 1986 through 1993, the thick-billed parrot was reintroduced in southern Arizona. The initial stock of 29 birds released in 1986 by the Arizona Game and Fish Department (AGFD), the U.S. Fish and Wildlife Service (FWS), and the U.S. Forest Service were comprised of parrots confiscated in smuggling attempts made from Mexico into the United States. Approximately 25 percent of these parrots were lost to birds of prey, another quarter were observed flying south toward Mexico, and 14 birds remained in Arizona. Over the next two years, of those birds remaining in Arizona, at least one pair nested and produced offspring. Although subsequent reintroductions were attempted, they were not sufficient to maintain a population in the wild. As a result of these reintroduction efforts, the current thick-billed parrot population consists of only a few birds.

The introduction of captive-bred parrots into the wild has not been successful. On release, these birds made little attempt to flock with the wild birds. Flocking behavior protects birds from predators so the hand-reared parrots made easy prey. A single, captive-reared bird raised by its parents was also released with this group. It immediately flocked with the wild group. Due to little success, however, captive-reared birds are not being considered for release in the wild.

The problem now facing the reintroduction program is obtaining a supply of wild parrots. Mexico is protecting its endangered and declining population, and confiscated birds are generally in poor condition. The AGFD, FWS, various Mexican cooperators, and the Wildlife Preservation Trust are coordinating efforts to locate enough wild parrots by the year 2000. These must be healthy enough to withstand removal for breeding and release in Arizona.

> ## The introduction of captive-bred parrots into the wild has not been successful.

Parrot

Monk seals comprise a genus of three similar, but geographically distinct species of seals. The Hawaiian monk seal is found almost exclusively around small, mostly uninhabited atolls and islands northwest of the main Hawaiian Islands. The rich marine life supplies this monk seal with an abundance of food, including fish, octopi, squid, and lobsters.

Hawaiian Monk

MONK SEALS COMPRISE A GENUS OF THREE SIMILAR, BUT GEOGRAPHICALLY DISTINCT SPECIES OF SEALS: THE HAWAIIAN, THE MEDITERRANEAN, AND THE CARIBBEAN. THE LATTER IS CONSIDERED EXTINCT AND THE FIRST TWO ARE IN DECLINE.

Researchers estimate current numbers to be between 1,300 and 1,400 for the Hawaiian monk seal and between 300 and 500 for the Mediterranean.

Most seals inhabit cool, northern waters. Monk seals are the only species found in warm, tropical and subtropical seas. The Hawaiian monk seal is found almost exclusively in the northwestern waters of the Hawaiian Islands. Its habitat is remote; few humans live on the islands that the monk seal calls home. These seals spend about one-third of their lives on land, and two-thirds in water. They haul themselves out of the water onto land to rest, give birth, and nurse their young. Monk seals are thought to feed in relatively shallow waters on reef fish, octopi, squid, and spiny lobsters, but they also feed over deeper waters, farther out to sea.

On land, Hawaiian monk seals have no natural predators. They are, however, easily disturbed by human visitors to their islands—an important factor in their decline. Human disturbance has caused pregnant females to give birth in poor habitat (where their pups are less likely to survive) or to abandon their newborns altogether.

In water, sharks are the monk seal's primary predators. Scientists do not know how often sharks kill seals, but many seals bear large scars, indicating that such attacks may be common. Scientists have collected pups and kept them in shark-proof enclosures until large enough to

The most significant problem facing the Hawaiian monk seal is the low survival rate of juveniles.

feed successfully on their own.

Male Hawaiian monk seals display a reproductive aggression that can be fatal or injurious to female or younger seals. This behavior is called "mobbing" and occurs when a group of males attempts to breed with a single female at the same time. Mobbing is thought to occur because, at some sites, adult males outnumber adult females. Attempts to reduce this behavior have recently focused on physical removal of males from these sites to even the sex ratio.

At present, the most significant problem facing the Hawaiian monk seal is the low survival rate of juveniles; many are simply starving to death. Scientists are trying to determine why these young seals are not finding enough food. They are also rehabilitating undersized animals for release at sites where food is more plentiful. Travel to these remote islands has been restricted as much of this monk seal's habitat is now part of a research site of the Hawaiian Islands National Wildlife Refuge. The National Marine Fisheries Service is leading the effort to recover the Hawaiian monk seal. Scientists have tagged and monitored over 1,000 seals in an attempt to better understand their habits and threats. Since 1985, the number of seals counted on beaches has declined by five percent per year, and recovery of these rare marine mammals will take a determined effort by scientists as well as a strong social commitment toward conservation.

Seal

The extreme southern tip of the Florida peninsula is, in fact, the northernmost range of the American crocodile. This large reptile is found in mangrove-lined, saltwater estuaries and swamps. The female nests along the banks of creeks or streams.

American

16

32 USA
American crocodile

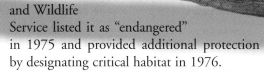

THE AMERICAN CROCODILE IS A LARGE, TROPICAL REPTILE WHICH INHABITS THE EXTREME SOUTHERN TIP OF THE FLORIDA PENINSULA. CROCODILES ARE SHY ANIMALS AND ARE EASILY DISTURBED BY HUMANS. IN FACT, NOT A SINGLE AMERICAN CROCODILE ATTACK ON A HUMAN HAS EVER BEEN RECORDED.

Although easily confused with the American alligator, crocodiles have a more triangular head and tapered snout with protruding teeth that give the appearance of a grin. Crocodiles are greyish-green and have a row of rigid, bony scales down their backs and smooth white scales on their bellies. From the tips of their snouts to the ends of their tails, male crocodiles can reach lengths of 15 feet while females attain lengths of 12 feet.

The American crocodile once inhabited saltwater, coastal wetlands along the Pacific Ocean from Mexico south to Ecuador, as well as along the Atlantic coast from Guatemala north to the extreme southern tip of Florida. Due to hunting for its hide and development of its habitat, the crocodile's numbers have declined dramatically. In the United States, the crocodile has been reduced to only three small, but stable populations in south Florida. To prevent further decline of this species, the U.S. Fish and Wildlife Service listed it as "endangered" in 1975 and provided additional protection by designating critical habitat in 1976.

Crocodiles spend the majority of the day resting in quiet waters of mangrove-lined swamps or in dens, which they build 10 to 30 feet into the banks of creeks or streams. At night they become more active and move to the water to feed. Fish, turtles, snakes, crabs, birds, and small mammals are their primary foods.

In March, the female begins looking for a nesting site, often returning to one she has used in the past. She scratches and digs to loosen the soil and, in late April or May, lays approximately 20 to 80 eggs and buries them in the nest. She returns periodically to her nest to listen for the activity that signals hatching. About 85 days after being laid, the eggs hatch. She helps her 10-inch-long offspring dig up through the soil and carries them to water where they are released. At this point, they are on their own. For a few weeks, the young crocodiles stay among the bankside vegetation, hiding from predators. During this period, they do not feed; instead they live off their remaining yolk sacs. After that, they move into protected wetlands and begin feeding—hungrily. Young American crocodiles grow faster than any other crocodile species, growing 16 to 20 inches a year.

To minimize disturbance to breeding crocodiles, some nesting sites have been closed to public access. Measures such as this, taken to protect the wary crocodile from humans, have been relatively successful. Numbers have increased steadily, from a low of only two dozen in the 1970s to more than 500 by 1990. The immediate recovery goal for the American crocodile is to improve its status from "endangered" to "threatened." This objective will be achieved once most of the current nesting areas yield surviving young crocodiles.

> *Due to hunting for its hide and development of its habitat, the crocodile's numbers have declined.*

Crocodile

Ocelots prefer to live in densely vegetated, secluded habitats. Once common in the southwestern United States, Mexico, and Central and South America, their numbers and range have been greatly reduced. In the U.S., an estimated 50 to 100 ocelots live in southernmost Texas.

18

THE OCELOT LIVES IN DENSELY VEGE-TATED HABITATS SUCH AS FORESTS, THICKETS, AND DESERT SCRUBLANDS. THIS SMALL, MUSCULAR CAT IS WELL ADAPTED TO THESE SECLUDED AREAS.

It can quietly slip through the thickest of vegetation, perfectly camouflaged in the dappled light that reaches the forest floor. Once a common resident in the southwestern United States, as well as Mexico and Central and South America, the ocelot's range and numbers have become greatly reduced. In the United States, this cat is now limited to southernmost Texas, where only 50 to 100 individuals are believed to exist.

The ocelot is a solitary animal. Like most cats, it is territorial, guarding its home from intruders. To define their territories, ocelots "scent mark" by spraying urine onto low vegetation. These marks warn other ocelots of the same sex to stay away. Ocelots prefer to travel and hunt under the cover of darkness. They feed primarily on rodents but will also hunt other small mammals, birds, reptiles, and even crabs.

Ocelots do not have a set breeding season and may produce kittens at any time of the year. Approximately 80 days after mating, the female gives birth to one or two kittens. They den in dark, secluded areas, such as caves, woodpiles, or clumps of grass. The kittens begin traveling with their mother by the time they are about three months old. They stay with her for about one year, learning hunting and other necessary sur-

Scientists are trying to learn more about these elusive cats.

vival skills. Sometime between the ages of one and three years old, the young cats will leave the shelter of their mother's territory and go off in search of a territory of their own.

Encroachment by man into the ocelot's once-secluded habitat is one reason for the ocelot's decline. As their habitat becomes divided by highways, killings by cars have become increasingly common. Another reason is the ocelot's beautiful fur, which has long been highly prized commercially. In the 1960s and 1970s, many paid up to $40,000 for a coat made from ocelot pelts. Many of these animals were hunted, trapped, and poisoned. Although the ocelot is now protected by the Endangered Species Act and other international protection agreements, some illegal hunting of these cats still occurs.

Currently, scientists are trying to learn more about these elusive cats so they can better manage and protect them. The U.S. Fish and Wildlife Service has funded studies on the south Texas ocelot population since 1981. These have focused on the ocelot's habitat and travel patterns. By attaching collars with radio transmitters onto a few animals, scientists can track their movements and learn more about the ocelot's behavior and mortality. Information gained from such research will be beneficial in formulating future strategies for saving this cat from extinction.

Ocelot

The Schaus swallowtail butterfly once ranged from the Miami area southward into the Florida Keys. Increased residential, commercial, and recreational development in south Florida has restricted the available habitat of this butterfly primarily to Key Biscayne National Park, Key Largo, and other islands within the Upper Keys.

Schaus Swallowtail

Schaus
swallowtail
butterfly

32
USA

THE SCHAUS SWALLOWTAIL IS A DARK BROWN AND YELLOW BUTTERFLY THAT ONCE RANGED FROM THE MIAMI AREA SOUTHWARD INTO THE FLORIDA KEYS, THE STRING OF TROPICAL ISLANDS AT THE SOUTHERNMOST TIP OF THE PENINSULA.

Increased development in south Florida has decreased this butterfly's habitat. Its distribution today is restricted primarily to Key Biscayne National Park, Key Largo, and other islands within the Upper Keys.

The Schaus is found only in undisturbed tropical "hammocks," which are areas of shrub and mature hardwood trees occurring in organic soil. The species depends on the vegetation within this habitat to support its life cycle. Adults feed on nectar from guava, cheese shrub, wild coffee blossoms, and other flowering plants. The leaves of torchwood and wild lime provide nutrition for the larval "caterpillars" and a place where the butterflies can sun themselves.

The Schaus is sometimes confused with other species of swallowtails whose ranges overlap within the Keys. The Schaus may be distinguished from these by its distinctive, half-diamond pattern of yellow stripes on a brown background, which occurs on the top of each set of wings. The undersides of the wings are mostly yellow, each with a prominent band of rusty-orange, edged with iridescent blue to the outside.

Like all butterflies, the Schaus swallowtail goes through several life stages. When its habitat is destroyed, each of these is adversely affected. The swallowtail begins life as an egg that the female lays on the leaves of its host plants. The larvae hatch after three to five days and begin feeding, concentrating on tender, new vegetation. After several "molts," or sheddings of its outer skin, the fully grown caterpillar attaches itself to a branch and changes into a "chrysalis," or pupa. This stage may last from six to twelve months, after which the adult butterfly emerges. Its adult life span is short though—only about two weeks.

Adult Schaus swallowtails do not migrate in large groups like some other butterflies. Individuals will, however, occasionally cross open water and reach other islands. This natural dispersal may aid in the species' survival by supplementing existing butterfly colonies or contributing to the establishment of new ones.

The habitat loss and threats from widespread mosquito spraying following increased residential development throughout the 1960s and 1970s led the U.S. Fish and Wildlife Service to list the Schaus swallowtail as "threatened" in 1976 and "endangered" in 1984. Since then, much progress has been made towards stabilizing and recovering the species. Some additional public land with appropriate butterfly habitat has been acquired, mosquito spraying has become more selective, and a captive breeding program has produced enough individual butterflies to begin small-scale reintroductions into their native environment. The outlook for the long-term survival of the Schaus swallowtail is improving with these efforts.

When its habitat is destroyed, each of its life stages is affected.

Butterfly

The Wyoming toad is the only toad found in the wetlands of south-eastern Wyoming's Laramie River basin. Once common throughout this area, it probably also inhabited similar marshlands nearby.

Wyoming

32 USA
Wyoming toad

22

THE WYOMING TOAD IS SMALL, ONLY ABOUT TWO INCHES LONG, WITH CRESTS ON ITS HEAD THAT FORM A RIDGE. ITS BROWN BODY IS COVERED WITH WARTS AND DARK BLOTCHES.

Unlike other toads, the Wyoming toad spends much of its time in water or marsh areas. It is only found in southeastern Wyoming's Laramie River basin.

Like all amphibians, the Wyoming toad begins life in a jelly-like egg that the female lays in shallow pools of water. Three to five days later, depending on water temperature, a tadpole emerges.

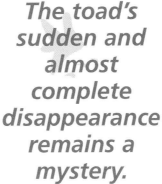

Immediately, the tadpole begins its transformation, or metamorphosis, into a toad. As a tadpole, it is potential prey for a large variety of fish and aquatic insects. The tadpole, in turn, feeds primarily on plant matter. Its hind legs develop first, then its front legs—but it still looks more like a fish than a toad. As its lungs develop, its tail shortens and gradually disappears. It then climbs out of the water and begins life as an adult toad. It preys on insects, larvae, and other small organisms found in its wetlands habitat.

Once common throughout the Laramie floodplains, the Wyoming toad probably also inhabited similar marshlands nearby. Fossil records suggest that the species was abundant thousands of years ago. Researchers from the University of Wyoming have been monitoring the toad's breeding sites since 1945. Numbers remained steady until 1978—when they dropped dramatically. Very few toads were counted after 1979.

Alarmed, scientists from the University of Wyoming and the U.S. Fish and Wildlife Service (FWS) began a comprehensive study of the entire Laramie River basin in 1980. Only a single population of toads was found, consisting of about 25 males.

No females, tadpoles, or eggs were found. In 1983, only two male toads were found, and in the following year, none. The Wyoming toad was believed extinct. Then, in 1987, a new population of approximately 150 toads was found in a two-square-mile area that contains Mortenson Lake. Scientists considered this population a good size for breeding and were optimistic about the toad's recovery.

The toad's sudden and almost complete disappearance remains a mystery. Because the leopard frog and boreal toad also experienced similar declines over the same period, some scientists believe the increased use of pesticides and herbicides is partly to blame. Malathion, a pesticide commonly used to combat mosquitoes, is known to cause mortality to toad eggs and their tadpoles. Pesticide use in and around known Wyoming toad populations will continue to be monitored by the Environmental Protection Agency.

Low reproduction rates and disease have caused the Wyoming toad's numbers to decline further. Redleg, a bacteria which all Wyoming toads are believed to carry, causes disease when triggered by stress. Environmental factors such as cold temperatures or human disturbance of habitat may bring about stress in these toads.

With the assistance of the Nature Conservancy, the FWS has acquired the majority of the existing toad habitat at Mortenson Lake. Measures to protect this population have been coordinated by the FWS and the Wyoming Game and Fish Department. Their objective is to maintain the existing population of approximately 200 adults and to establish viable populations of approximately 100 adults each in five other nearby locations.

The toad's sudden and almost complete disappearance remains a mystery.

Toad

There are two similar subspecies of brown pelicans in the United States: the California brown pelican, which lives primarily along the southern California coast but can also be found in Oregon and Washington State, and the Eastern brown pelican, which inhabits areas along the southern Atlantic and Gulf coasts.

Brown

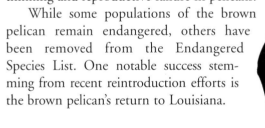

THE BROWN PELICAN'S MOST FAMOUS FEATURE IS ITS LARGE THROAT POUCH. SUSPENDED FROM THE BOTTOM OF A LONG AND SLENDER BILL, THE POUCH CAN HOLD UP TO THREE TIMES MORE THAN THE STOMACH.

Pelicans use the pouch as a net to scoop fish up from the sea. After draining the water—up to three gallons-worth—the pelican may transport the meal home for its chicks. There the hungry chicks use the pouch as a feeding trough.

The brown pelican's range was once extensive, encompassing areas along the Atlantic, Pacific, and Gulf coasts of North America and the Caribbean coasts of Central and South America. In the United States, there are two similar subspecies: the California brown pelican, which lives on the west coast, primarily along the southern California coast; and the Eastern brown pelican, which inhabits the Atlantic coast from the Carolinas southward and westward along the Gulf of Mexico.

Brown pelicans rarely venture either far inland or far out to sea. They are extremely social birds, often seen flying in large flocks, necks folded, heads resting on their backs, their muscular wings slowly beating. With keen eyesight, pelicans can spot small fish from heights of 60 to 70 feet. Upon sighting a meal, the pelican dives steeply into the water, then resurfaces, often with a pouchful of fish. A single bird requires up to four pounds of fish per day.

Good swimmers and strong flyers, pelicans seem clumsy, almost comical, on land due to their large size. They prefer small, inaccessible coastal islands as breeding sites where they con-

gregate in large colonies. Depending on the topography and materials available, their nests may be shallow, feather-lined depressions in sand or soil or treetop platforms built of reeds and grasses. In the spring, females usually lay three eggs which both sexes take turns incubating. The young are hatched naked and helpless, and develop down feathers after 10 days. They mature quickly; in about 12 weeks they are fully feathered and ready to leave the nest.

This large, fish-eating bird was once such a fixture of the Gulf landscape that in 1803 Louisiana's governor chose the brown pelican as its state bird, placing it prominently on both the state flag and seal. In the 1930s, an estimated 60,000 birds nested on Louisiana's offshore islands, but 20 years later its numbers had dropped dramatically. This resulted in pelicans abandoning their last-known Louisiana nesting site, making Louisiana the first state to experience the loss of its official bird.

Pesticides were the primary cause of the pelican's decline throughout the United States. DDT and other toxins accumulated in the waterways and passed from fish to fowl. DDT was associated with eggshell thinning and reproductive failure in pelicans.

While some populations of the brown pelican remain endangered, others have been removed from the Endangered Species List. One notable success stemming from recent reintroduction efforts is the brown pelican's return to Louisiana.

Pesticides were the primary cause of the pelican's decline.

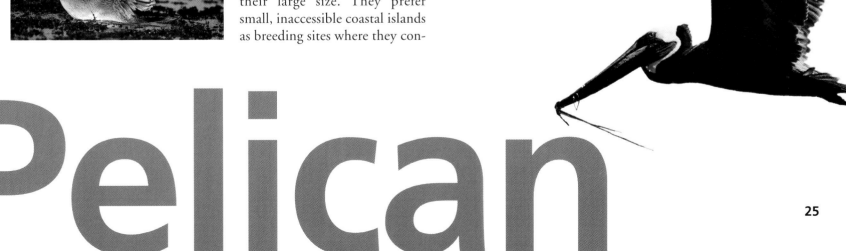

Pelican

Fossil records show that 100,000 years ago, the California condor ranged over much of western North America and eastward, along the U.S./Mexico border to Florida. Causes for the decrease in range and population of this scavenging bird are numerous, and in early 1996, only 103 California condors existed in the world, 17 in the wild and 86 in breeding facilities.

California

T HE CALIFORNIA CONDOR, NORTH AMERICA'S LARGEST BIRD, IS AMONG THE LARGEST FLYING BIRDS IN THE WORLD. A FULL-GROWN ADULT CAN WEIGH 20 POUNDS AND HAVE A WINGSPAN OF 10 FEET.

Over semi-arid landscapes, the California condor soars using its large wings. Black-and-white feathers and an orange-colored head make the condor stand out against the sky. It was known to many North American Indian tribes as the "thunderbird," a messenger to their ancestors and spirits.

Today, the California condor still inspires awe. Its large, muscular wings are well suited for flying over the deep, rocky canyons of its habitat in the foothills and mountains of southern California. It can attain speeds of 50 miles per hour and may fly 140 miles per day in search of food. Like all vultures, the California condor is a scavenger, feeding on carcasses of dead animals such as cattle, deer, elk, and pronghorn. Occasionally it will consume smaller animals such as rodents and fish.

The California condor was never numerous. Fossil records show that 100,000 years ago, it ranged over much of western North America, from British Columbia to Baja California, and eastward along the U.S./Mexico border to Florida. Until about 2,000 years ago, condors lived in Texas, Arizona, and New Mexico. They were present in the Pacific Northwest until the 1800s, and in northern Baja California until the early 1930s. The entire population of California condors numbered about 60 birds in the 1960s and dwindled to only 21 to 24 in the 1980s.

Causes for this decline are many and condor deaths have exceeded births. Because they are scav-

The future of the California condor lies with the success— or failure—of breeding and release programs.

engers, condors often consume the remains of animals that may contain fragments of bullets that can cause lead poisoning. As cities and towns have diminished the condor's habitat, condors have had fatal collisions with power lines. Ingestion of carcasses with high levels of pesticides also has contributed to condor deaths.

Early federal efforts beginning in 1937, such as closing nesting areas to the public and restricting air and road traffic, did little to stop the condor's decline. With about 15 condors left in the wild, the American Ornithologists' Union and the National Audubon Society began an aggressive study in 1980 that proposed restocking the wild population with captive-bred birds. Then disaster struck: nine of the fifteen remaining birds vanished between November 1984 and April 1985. With extinction of the species a real possibility, the U.S. Fish and Wildlife Service undertook a controversial program of trapping and bringing into captivity all of the remaining condors.

In April 1988, the first chick ever conceived in captivity was hatched at California's San Diego Zoo. Over the next few years, 37 condors were bred and reintroduced in the wild—but not without high mortality rates. Four died after colliding with power lines and one died from ingesting poisons. Another 15 were captured and brought back to captivity because their behavior, such as perching on power lines, was too risky. They just did not have the survival skills of wild birds. Release studies using captive-bred Andean condors, a more common relative of the California condor, are now underway. As of May 1996, 115 California condors existed in the world, with 17 in the wild and 98 in breeding facilities. Today, there is little doubt that the future of the California condor lies with the success—or failure—of breeding and release programs.

Condor

Formerly common throughout New Mexico's Gila and San Francisco Rivers, and in Arizona's Agua Fria and Verde Rivers, the Gila trout's numbers have declined significantly. Recovery efforts, begun in 1978, have been successful, and the Gila population has been restored in seven designated wilderness habitats in New Mexico.

Gila

28

Gila trout
32
USA

THE GILA TROUT IS READILY DISTINGUISHED FROM OTHER RELATED SPECIES BY ITS IRIDESCENT GOLDEN SIDES, WHICH DARKEN TO COPPER ON THE GILL COVERS. IRREGULAR SPOTS COVER THE SIDES AND BACK. DURING SPAWNING SEASON, THE GILA TROUT'S WHITE BELLY BECOMES STREAKED WITH ORANGE OR YELLOW.

The Gila trout was once abundant in New Mexico's Gila and San Francisco Rivers as well as in Arizona's Verde and Agua Fria Rivers. These rivers and their tributaries, with their moderate currents and deep pools, provided refuge from the region's severe droughts. In these waters, the Gila fed on insects such as water beetles, flies, dragonflies, mayflies, caddis flies, ants, and aquatic insect larvae.

By the 1960s, the number of Gila trout declined rapidly; it even became extinct in Arizona. By the late 1970s, the Gila had vanished from all but five streams in New Mexico. The region's waterways had become polluted, sport fishing had increased dramatically, and the Gila produced hybrid offspring after breeding with introduced, non-native trout. The damming, draining, and rerouting of preferred rivers to make way for urban development also led to the trout's demise.

Many recovery efforts since 1978 have concentrated on preventing the hybridization of the Gila trout primarily with non-native rainbow trout. Preferred habitats were identified and non-native trout relocated to other streams. These higher quality areas were then restocked with pure Gila from the wild.

This strategy has created streams where Gila trout are once again the dominant species of trout. As their numbers increased, the Gila naturally expanded into other streams and rivers. By the end of 1987, scientists had restored the Gila to seven designated wilderness habitat within New Mexico's Gila National Forest. Recently, the U.S. Fish and Wildlife Service transferred 36 adult fish and 1,800 eggs to a hatchery in New Mexico as part of another captive breeding program aimed at restocking the Gila into larger streams.

If such efforts continue to be successful, the Gila's status may be changed from "endangered" to "threatened." Sport fishing, currently banned as part of the recovery effort, may even be reinstated as the numbers of Gila trout reach the maximum limits that their river habitats can sustain.

> **Recovery efforts have concentrated on preventing the hybridization of the Gila trout.**

Trout

Although the range of the San Francisco garter snake has always been narrow, today it has been diminished even further. This colorful snake survives in about 20 isolated areas of California's San Francisco Bay area.

San Francisco Garter

THE SAN FRANCISCO GARTER SNAKE IS BRIGHTLY COLORED WITH RED, BLACK, AND GREENISH YELLOW STRIPES RUNNING DOWN ITS BACK. THE TOP OF ITS HEAD IS RED, AND ITS BELLY IS GREENISH BLUE; BUT FOR ALL ITS BRILLIANT COLOR, IT IS HARMLESS TO HUMANS.

In fact, it is an extremely shy reptile, fleeing into water or nearby brush when disturbed. It requires wetland habitats for survival and is most often found in and around ponds, lakes, and marshes. On land, the snake seeks protection in bankside vegetation such as cattails, bulrushes, and spike rushes. Using implanted radio transmitters, studies have shown that this snake lives its entire life within 600 feet of water.

It depends on wetlands for food because its diet consists heavily of amphibians and fish. Red-legged frogs, Pacific tree frogs, immature California newts, and western toads are favorites, as are threespine stickleback and mosquito fish.

This snake's geographic range is narrow, and its name comes from its only habitat, California's San Francisco Bay area. This brightly striped snake was once found throughout the San Francisco Peninsula from the San Francisco County line south through San Mateo County to Año Nuevo Point. It inhabited lowlands along both the western and eastern foothills of the Santa Cruz Mountains. Today, it survives only at about 20 isolated locations within this historic range.

Fragmentation of the garter snake's habitat has led its populations to become isolated and inbred. Inbreeding can result in a serious reduction of fitness, loss of fertility, and increased susceptibility to disease and genetic abnormalities. Human development of the garter snake's habitat is another threat. Streams have been dried up or diverted, bankside vegetation eliminated, and large tracts of wetlands developed. This has driven the San Francisco garter snake into ever-diminishing pockets of remaining habitat.

Another threat to the snake is illegal trade. Collectors and dealers prize the garter snake's skin for its beautiful coloring. The U.S. Fish and Wildlife Service (FWS) is responsible for enforcing laws against killing or removing endangered species from the wild. The FWS also manages four conservation areas in the San Francisco Bay area for the protection of other species. These areas indirectly protect certain populations of the San Francisco garter snake. The agency's goal is to expand protection to at least 10 populations, with each consisting of about 200 adult snakes. Once a combined population of about 2,000 snakes can be maintained for five consecutive years, the FWS will consider reclassifying the San Francisco garter snake from "endangered" to "threatened."

Fragmentation of the garter snake's habitat has led its populations to become isolated and inbred.

Snake

When North America was first settled, the woodland caribou ranged throughout mature forests from New England westward to Washington State. Today, with diminished habitat, the endangered United States caribou populations are confined to a small area spanning the Idaho and Washington border.

32

Woodland

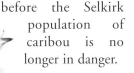

THE WOODLAND CARIBOU INHABITS COLD, MOUNTAINOUS TERRAIN. ITS LARGE HOOVES ACT LIKE SNOWSHOES, ALLOWING IT TO TREK ATOP THE SNOW WITHOUT SINKING MORE THAN A FEW INCHES.

Even when the snow mounts to 15 to 20 feet, the caribou can reach the upper branches of evergreen trees to feed on lichen. This adaptation has sustained the woodland caribou in areas that may be snow-covered up to six months per year.

Large expanses of mature forests once covered much of the northern United States from New England to Washington State. When North America was first settled, woodland caribou were commonly seen throughout this range. Dense forests of fir, spruce, cedar, aspen, and hemlock provided the caribou with adequate shelter and seemingly unlimited food. By 1900, however, the woodland caribou survived mainly from Montana westward and in western Canada and Alaska. These populations also declined as loggers cleared much of the region's forests. Disease, fires, and beetles killed many of the remaining trees. One remnant group of caribou on the Idaho and Montana border died out in the 1950s. By 1960 a once-numerous population in the mountains of eastern Washington and Idaho was reduced to just 100 animals. Today, only about 50 to 70 woodland caribou still survive in the Selkirk Mountains of southern British Columbia and northern Idaho, and in northeastern Washington State. (Farther north, however, these animals are still relatively numerous and not con-sidered endangered. An estimated 1.1 million inhabit wilderness areas of Alaska and northwestern British Columbia.)

The states of Idaho and Washington are working with the U.S. Fish and Wildlife Service (FWS) to manage the remaining U.S. caribou populations. Efforts focus on maintaining and increasing existing populations, and on securing and enhancing caribou habitat in Washington and Idaho. Hunters sometimes mistake the caribou for the more common deer or elk, and campaigns to inform them of the caribou's presence have prevented several caribou deaths.

Much of the caribou's range lies within areas administered by the U.S. Forest Service. The FWS and the Canadian Wildlife Service have recommended restoring the caribou's habitat by restricting, but not eliminating, logging. Felling trees throughout the caribou's winter feeding grounds will be severely limited.

From 1987 to 1990, woodland caribou were taken from Canada and relocated to northern Idaho. These efforts have been relatively successful but numbers are still low. Scientists estimate that it will take many years of population management before the Selkirk population of caribou is no longer in danger.

> **Much of the caribou's range lies within areas administered by the FWS.**

Caribou

The Florida panther once ranged throughout the American southeast, from the lower Mississippi River Valley eastward to Florida and the Atlantic coast. Today, this species survives only in the subtropical swamps and forestlands of southern Florida.

Florida

Florida panther

32
USA

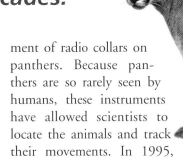

AS FLORIDA'S OFFICIAL STATE ANIMAL, THE PANTHER HAS BECOME A SYMBOL FOR PROTECTING THE EVERGLADES AND OTHER SENSITIVE ENVIRONMENTS OF SOUTHERN FLORIDA. THIS MAJESTIC FELINE IS USED ON ADVERTISING—EVEN LICENSE PLATES— TO PROMOTE THE STATE'S CONSERVATION EFFORTS, AND WITH GOOD REASON:

The Florida panther is one of the most endangered mammals on earth. Only 30 to 50 adults are believed to survive in the wild, in a habitat that has been diminishing for decades. The Florida panther once ranged throughout the American southeast, from the lower Mississippi River Valley eastward to Florida and the Atlantic coast. Today, this species survives only in the subtropical swamps and forestlands of southern Florida.

To thrive, an adult male panther may require 200 to 300 square miles of territory, which it defends against other male panthers. This habitat must be secluded and free of excessive human activity, which is why the panther's range has diminished. Development in south Florida has increased dramatically over the last few decades as human populations have more than tripled. Vast areas of wetlands have been drained to facilitate residential, commercial, and agricultural expansion. Native forests have been cleared or bisected by roads and highways. Connecting Naples with Ft. Lauderdale, one

Only 30 to 50 adult panthers are believed to survive in the wild, in a habitat that has been diminishing for decades.

such highway, known as Alligator Alley, runs right through prime panther habitat. Several panthers have been struck and killed by automobiles on this and other roads.

At present, the Florida panther is found only in south Florida. Its low numbers and somewhat fragmented population complicate the panther's chances for survival. Because its numbers are so low, "inbreeding," or mating among closely related individuals, is occurring. Offspring produced from inbreeding are likely to be more susceptible to disease, have problems reproducing, or suffer from other health problems.

To address these trends, the U.S. Fish and Wildlife Service, the National Park Service, the Florida Game and Fresh Water Fish Commission, and the Florida Department of Environmental Protection began a cooperative recovery program in 1986. Part of the effort involves the placement of radio collars on panthers. Because panthers are so rarely seen by humans, these instruments have allowed scientists to locate the animals and track their movements. In 1995, eight female Texas cougars, a species closely related to the Florida panther, were released in south Florida in an attempt to reduce inbreeding and restore genetic health to the panther. Several kittens have since been born, and the program appears to be working well.

Panther

The piping plover exists in three separate populations: one along the Atlantic coast and the other two in the upper Great Lakes and the northern Great Plains. It winters along the Atlantic and Gulf coasts and into the Bahamas and West Indies. The plover is among the first migratory birds to return to its breeding grounds each March.

Piping

THE PIPING PLOVER'S MELODIOUS, BELL-LIKE WHISTLES ALERT ALL TO THIS SHOREBIRD'S PRESENCE, EVEN WHEN IT IS WELL CAMOUFLAGED. IT IS STOCKY IN BUILD WITH A SHORT BILL.

Its plumage is pale beige above and white below, with a single black chest band and crown patch, thus blending well with the sandy beaches of a favored habitat. The plover exists in three separate breeding populations: one along the Atlantic coast, another in the Great Lakes area, and the third in the northern Great Plains. Piping plovers winter along the Atlantic and Gulf coasts and into the Bahamas and West Indies.

Come spring they return to their breeding grounds. Once nesting territories are established and courtship rituals completed, each pair then forms a depression in the sand or gravel on the beach. Sometimes these birds use small stones or shell fragments to line their "nests." Up to four eggs hatch in about four weeks, and the flightless young are soon able to follow their parents in foraging for aquatic worms, insects, and amphipods. Both eggs and young are so well camouflaged that they are apt to be undetected unless stepped on. Young are able to fly at around 30 days of age.

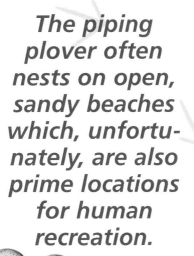

Loss and degradation of habitat due to development have been major reasons for the plover's decline. Construction of dams and reservoirs on the Missouri River and its tributaries has drastically altered water flow patterns, permanently inundating some habitats and increasing flooding during nesting season. Dredging of waterways also poses severe threats to the plover's wintering habitat, especially on the Gulf coast.

The piping plover often nests on open, sandy beaches which, unfortunately, are also prime locations for human recreation.

Litter left by visitors attracts predators such as raccoons and foxes as well as unleashed dogs and cats. The plover's ground-dwelling nests make easy targets for these predators. Nests are sometimes also crushed by pedestrian or vehicular traffic. Excessive disturbance may interrupt the feeding of chicks, and adults may abandon their nests. While the plover's numbers have declined dramatically due to the presence of humans, other species such as large gulls, have benefited due to the increased availability of human-supplied food.

The U.S. Fish and Wildlife Service and local agencies have taken several steps to protect the once numerous piping plover. These birds are designated "endangered" in the Great Lakes area, where only 40 adult birds remain. The birds are considered "threatened" on the Northern Great Plains and Atlantic coast, where U.S. populations hover at around 2,300 and 1,700 adults, respectively. Federal and state natural resource agencies, local governments, and private organizations post certain areas closed to humans during the nesting and chick-rearing season. In several states, entire beachfronts of natural parks are blocked off to provide peaceful foraging and breeding sites for the plover. Laws restricting recreational vehicles and dogs are now common on beaches throughout the plover's range.

By learning to recognize and avoid these rare birds, leaving pets at home, and carrying trash and food scraps off the beach, humans can increase the chances for future generations of piping plovers.

> ## *The piping plover often nests on open, sandy beaches which, unfortunately, are also prime locations for human recreation.*

Plover

In the United States, the Florida manatee is found year-round along the Florida coast. During the summer, it is occasionally found from coastal Virginia to Louisiana along the Gulf of Mexico. This manatee is also seen off the northeast coast of South America and among the islands of the Caribbean.

Florida

T HE FLORIDA MANATEE SPENDS MUCH OF ITS TIME FLOATING JUST BELOW THE WATER'S SURFACE. ITS WHISKER-COVERED SNOUT MAY BE THE ONLY THING VISIBLE AS IT CHOMPS ON AQUATIC VEGETATION SUCH AS HYDRILLA, HYACINTH, AND SEA GRASS.

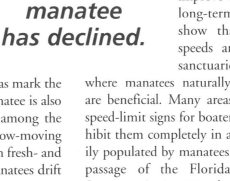

A manatee must eat up to 10 percent of its weight each day to fuel its massive body. This may mean 100 pounds of plants per day for a mature adult. Most full-grown manatees reach lengths of approximately 10 feet and weigh between 800 and 1,000 pounds, although males as long as 12 feet and weighing up to 3,500 pounds have been recorded. The manatee's fatty, grey-brown body resembles that of the walrus.

In the United States, the Florida manatee is found throughout the year along the Florida coast. In summer, some animals migrate northward and can be found from the Louisiana coast on the Gulf of Mexico to coastal Virgina. On rare occasions, manatees have been spotted in the Chesapeake Bay and farther north. As soon as the weather begins to cool, however, they return to their subtropical homeland. In fact, the U.S. coastal areas mark the northern limits of the manatee's range. The Florida manatee is also found off the northeast coast of South America and among the islands of the Caribbean. Manatees prefer broad, slow-moving rivers and shallow, coastal bays, and move freely between fresh- and saltwater. With easy strokes of their paddlelike tails, manatees drift from cove to cove looking for food.

Ever since humans have shared the manatee's habitat, the manatee has declined. Native Americans hunted the manatee for food and used its bones for making tools. The early European settlers also ate the animal's flesh and used its fat as lamp oil. Defenseless, the lumbering manatee made easy prey. Such hunting is believed

Ever since humans have shared the manatee's habitat, the manatee has declined.

largely responsible for the manatee's initial decline in numbers. Since 1907, there has been a $500 fine—and possible jail sentence—for anyone found guilty of killing or harming a manatee. After an all-time low in the 1940s, the manatee population increased to about 1,000 in 1970 and to almost 2,600 in 1996.

Humans are still the manatee's biggest threat—not with our spears, but with our speedboats. Because manatees are generally not visible as they float just below the water's surface, speeding boats often hit them. If not killed outright, manatees are often seriously injured; the propeller blades slice through their backs. Because almost all of Florida's manatees carry scars from such encounters, these are now used by scientists as a way of identifying and tracking individual animals.

In 1988 scientists from the U.S. Fish and Wildlife Service, the National Ecology Research Center, (now the National Biological Service), and the Florida Department of Environmental Protection initiated studies to improve the manatee's chances for long-term survival. Findings show that slowing boat speeds and establishing sanctuaries in places where manatees naturally congregate are beneficial. Many areas now post speed-limit signs for boaters and prohibit them completely in areas heavily populated by manatees. With the passage of the Florida Manatee Sanctuary Act in 1978, the entire state has been designated a refuge and sanctuary for the manatee. With increased awareness and positive actions such as these, the manatee's future may be brighter.

Manatee

Acknowledgments:

These stamps were produced by Stamp Services, United States Postal Service.

Marvin Runyon, *Postmaster General and Chief Executive Officer*
Loren Smith, *Chief Marketing Officer and Senior Vice President*
Azeezaly S. Jaffer, *Manager, Stamp Services*

Contributors:

Valoree S. Vargo, Manager, *Stamp and Product Marketing*
Andrew L. Gunn Wilinski, *Project Manager*
Carl Eichorn, *Printing Supervisor*
Author: Wayne Kurie, Supon Design Group, Washington, D.C.
Designer: Deborah N. Savitt, Supon Design Group, Washington, D.C.
Art Director, Stamps: Dick Sheaff, R. Dana Sheaff & Company
Designer, Stamps: James Balog, using Mamiya cameras and Kodak EPP film.
Editorial Consultant: Maria Mudd Ruth
Visual and Editorial Research: PhotoAssist, Inc.

Assistance:

Background information from *The Official World Wildlife Fund Guide to Endangered Species of North America,* Beacham Publishing, Inc., Washington, DC, 1990.

Personnel of the national, regional, and field offices of Ecological Services, U.S. Fish and Wildlife Service.

Map Directional:

The shaded states on each map are explained in the corresponding map legend and page text.

Photograph Credits:
t=top, b=bottom, c=center, l=left, r=right

Aerie Nature Series:
17tr, 27tr © W. Perry Conway

Animals, Animals:
35tr © Ken Cole; 14c © Victoria de Bettencourt; 33tr © Francis Lepine; 17tl © Ted Levin; 15br © Bates Littlehales; 33tl © Brian Milne; 31bl © Frank Schneidermeyer; 36c, 37c © Perry Slocum; 32c © Ed Wolff

Butterfly World:
20c © Ronald Boender

DRK Photo:
13br © John Cancalosi; 16c © James R. Fisher; 35bl © Steve Kaufman; 25br © Stephen J. Krasemann; 17bl © Tom and Pat Leeson; 19tr © Wayne Lynch; 39tr © Doug Perrine

Earth Views:
cover bc © Stanley M. Minasian

Minden Pictures:
15bl, 15tr, 25tr, 35br © Frans Lanting
8bl © Larry Minden

Photo Researchers Inc.:
39br © Douglas Faulkner

cover tr, cover br, cover c, 6tr, 9r, 21br, 37br © James Balog

19bl, 24c © Tom Boyden

21bl, 21tr © Thomas C. Emmel

19tl, 26c © Jeff Foott

27br © François Gohier

34c © John and Karen Hollingsworth

28c, 29br, 29br © David Propst

cover bl, 12c, 13bl, 13tr, 25bl, 37tl, 37tr, 38c, 39tl © Robert Rattner

29tl, 29tr © John Rinne

30c, 31tr, 31r © Michael Sewell

18c, 19br © Wendy Shattil/Bob Rozinski

27bl © Helen Snyder

cover tl, 7br, 10c, 11tr, 11br, 11bl, 22c, 23tr, 23br, 23l © Jeff Vanuga

33br © Art Wolff